DATE DUE FOR RETURN

KU-040-672

SK

ALPHA BOOKS

1960s

Nicola Barber

Evans

EVANS BROTHERS LIMITED

LU 14915502

LIVERPOOL LIBRARIES

Contents

SK 26/1/2000

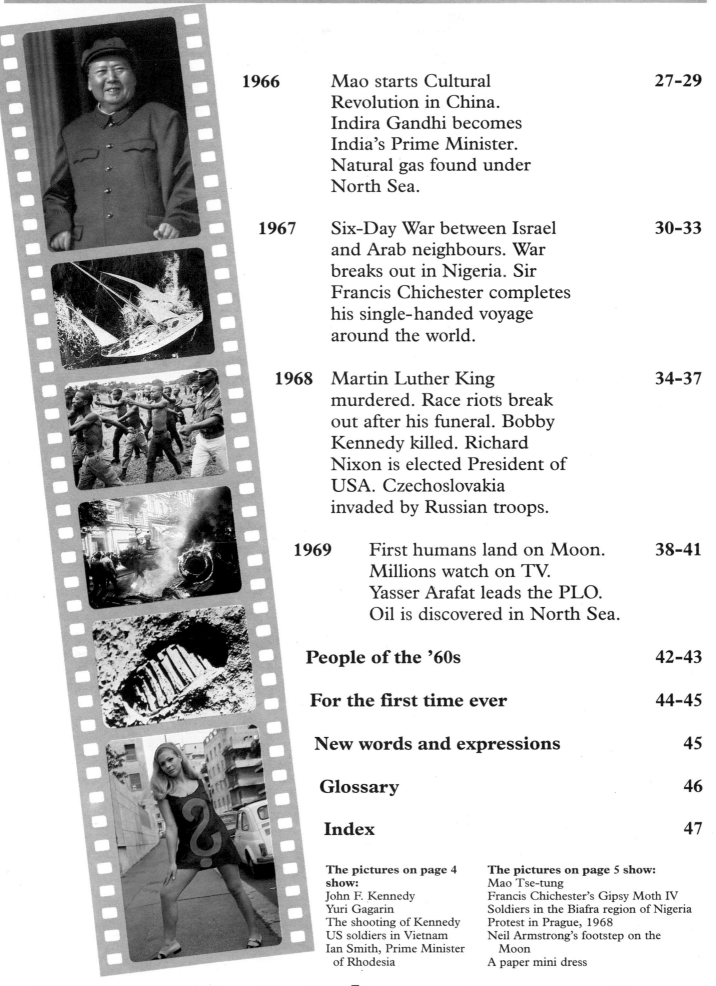

The pictures on page 4 show:
John F. Kennedy
Yuri Gagarin
The shooting of Kennedy
US soldiers in Vietnam
Ian Smith, Prime Minister of Rhodesia

The pictures on page 5 show:
Mao Tse-tung
Francis Chichester's Gipsy Moth IV
Soldiers in the Biafra region of Nigeria
Protest in Prague, 1968
Neil Armstrong's footstep on the Moon
A paper mini dress

Introduction

In the 1960s, the two most powerful countries in the world were the United States of America (the USA) and Russia (the USSR). These two countries did not trust each other. Both countries had stocks of nuclear weapons. In 1962 they nearly went to war against each other. The whole world waited in fear while the two sides decided what to do. At last, the two countries came to an agreement. For the time being, the threat of a nuclear war was over.

There were many wars throughout the 1960s. America sent soldiers to fight Communism in Vietnam. The Israelis and the Arabs fought a Six-Day war. There were also wars in Nigeria and Cyprus.

In other parts of the world, people were protesting. In America, black people struggled to get equal rights with white people. In South Africa, the black leader Nelson Mandela was jailed. Russian troops marched into Prague, the capital of Czechoslovakia, to stop protests against Communist rule. In Germany, the East Germans built a wall across the middle of Berlin to stop people escaping from the Communist East.

The 1960s ended with a triumph. The first men walked on the surface of the Moon and returned safely to Earth.

YEARS	WORLD AFFAIRS
1960	USA-USSR meeting in Paris Nigerian independence
1961	East Germans flee to the West East Germans close border at Berlin US and USSR test nuclear weapons
1962	USSR sends missiles to Cuba USA stops Russian ships sailing into Cuba Threat of war averted
1963	J. F. Kennedy killed in Dallas, Texas
1964	Lyndon B. Johnson elected US president Palestine Liberation Organization founded China tests atom bomb
1965	Rhodesia declares independence UK blocks trade with Rhodesia
1966	Cultural Revolution in China India elects Indira Gandhi
1967	Tension in Middle East Six-Day War gives Israel new territory Army officers seize power in Greece
1968	Czechoslovakia's 'Prague Spring' crushed Richard Nixon elected US President
1969	

WARS & REVOLTS	PEOPLE	EVENTS
Protestors killed in Sharpeville, South Africa Revolt in Algeria	Gary Powers admits spying mission J. F. Kennedy elected as US President Prime Minister Verwoerd shot in South Africa	US spyplane shot down over USSR Rome Olympic Games
British troops defend Kuwait Arabs guard Kuwait Bay of Pigs Cuban invasion fails	Yuri Gagarin in space	J. F. Kennedy sworn in as US President
Race riots in Mississippi	John Glenn becomes the first American in space Marilyn Monroe dies Nelson Mandela jailed American painter Andy Warhol exhibits Pop Art	New Coventry Cathedral opened First hovercraft service
	Profumo scandal in London Pope John XXIII dies	Great Train Robbery Beeching Report cuts British trains
US send troops to Vietnam	Martin Luther King wins Nobel Peace Prize Mandela jailed for life Nehru dies	Tokyo Olympic Games Cassius Clay wins heavyweight boxing title
Race riots in USA More US troops sent to Vietnam	Sir Winston Churchill dies	Civil rights demonstration in USA End of death penalty in UK
US attack in Vietnam Australian troops go to Vietnam	Francis Chichester knighted Prime Minister Verwoerd murdered	Aberfan tragedy in Wales England wins World Cup Labour wins UK election
Nigerian civil war Vietnam war continued Six-Day war between Israel and Arab states	Donald Campbell dies in accident Sir Francis Chichester sails home	Concorde unveiled Festival of Love Heart transplant
Riots in US after King's murder Nigerian war continues; Biafrans defeated	Martin Luther King murdered Yuri Gagarin dies Bobby Kennedy murdered	Mexico Olympic Games US astronaut orbits Moon
	Neil Armstrong and Edwin Aldrin walk on the Moon Yasser Arafat leads PLO	*Apollo 11* mission lands men on the Moon North Sea oil discovered

1960

Meeting for peace

May 2, Moscow, USSR In two weeks' time, there will be an important meeting in Paris, France. The meeting will be between Mr Khrushchev, the leader of the USSR, and President Eisenhower of the USA. The two superpowers do not trust each other. Both countries have nuclear weapons. If they went to war it would affect the whole world. So Khrushchev and Eisenhower are meeting to discuss ways to end the distrust between the two countries.

Russians shoot down US plane

May 10, Moscow, USSR The Russians have shot down a US plane. The plane was flying over Russia when it was hit. The pilot was not hurt when the plane crashed. He has admitted that he was spying for the American government.

The American spy pilot, Gary Powers, on trial in Moscow

End to peace talks

May 17, Paris, France The US will not apologise to the USSR about the spy plane. As a result, the Russians will not discuss peace with the Americans. The hostility between the two superpowers is often called the Cold War. Today, the Cold War looks as if it will continue.

LIVERPOOL LIBRARIES &

Unrest in South Africa

March 21, Johannesburg, South Africa
South African police killed 67 people and injured nearly 200 at Sharpeville, near Johannesburg. The dead and injured people were black Africans. They had gathered to protest about the South African pass laws. These laws force every black African to carry an identity card all

Armed police walk among the bodies of dead protesters at Sharpeville.

the time. The South African government has also put many black African leaders into prison to stop them speaking out against apartheid. Apartheid is a law that keeps people of different races apart and does not give them equal rights.

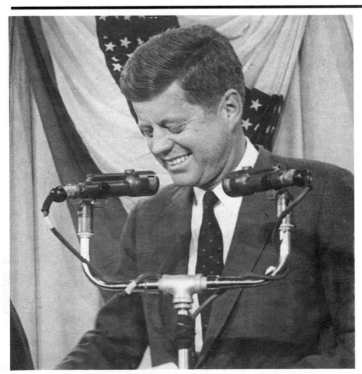

America elects youngest president

November 9, Washington DC, USA The Americans have elected John F. Kennedy as their new president. Kennedy is leader of the Democrat party. He defeated the leader of the Republican party, Richard Nixon, by only 120,000 votes. John F. Kennedy is 43 years old. He will be the youngest president ever to lead the United States.

A smile from John F. Kennedy after he wins the presidential election

Rebels in Algeria

February 1, Paris, France President de Gaulle of France has prevented civil war in the African country of Algeria. Algeria is a French colony, and many people from France have settled there. The French government is now planning to make Algeria an independent country once again. The settlers did not like this idea, and tried to rebel against the French army in Algeria. But after a television speech by President de Gaulle, the army forced the rebels to surrender peacefully.

News in brief...

Record Rome Olympics

September 4, Rome, Italy A record 5337 people took part in the Olympic Games in Rome. This makes these Olympics the biggest ever. The USA and the USSR won the most medals. But the star of the Games was the Australian runner, Herb Elliott. He won the 1500 metres race in world-record time.

The Australian Herb Elliott wins the 1500 metres in Rome.

US pilot found guilty

August 19, Moscow, USSR A court in the USSR has found the US pilot, Gary Powers, guilty of spying. He is sentenced to ten years in prison.

Independence for Nigeria

October 1, Lagos, Nigeria At midnight last night, Nigeria became independent. Nigeria was a British colony.

South African leader shot

April 9, Johannesburg, South Africa An attacker has shot the leader of the South African government, Prime Minister Verwoerd. The attacker was a rich, white farmer called David Pratt. Doctors think that Prime Minister Verwoerd will recover. Many white South Africans are very shocked that a white man has carried out such an act of violence.

1961

East Germans flee to West

July 31, Berlin, East Germany Every month, more than 30,000 people leave East Germany and go to the West to start new lives. They make the crossing from East to West in the city of Berlin. The city lies in East Germany, but it is divided into two parts, East and West Berlin. The Communist government controls East Berlin. France, Britain and the USA control West Berlin.

A wall divides East from West

August 23, Berlin, East Germany Ten days ago, the East German government closed the crossing points between East and West Berlin. No one was allowed to go from East to West. Now the East Germans are building a wall to divide the city in two. The wall is to stop East Germans escaping to the West.

The East Germans build up the wall between East and West Berlin.

Kennedy becomes president

January 20, Washington DC, USA John F. Kennedy made his first speech as president today. He told Americans: "Ask not what your country can do for you, ask what you can do for your country."

The new president makes his first speech.

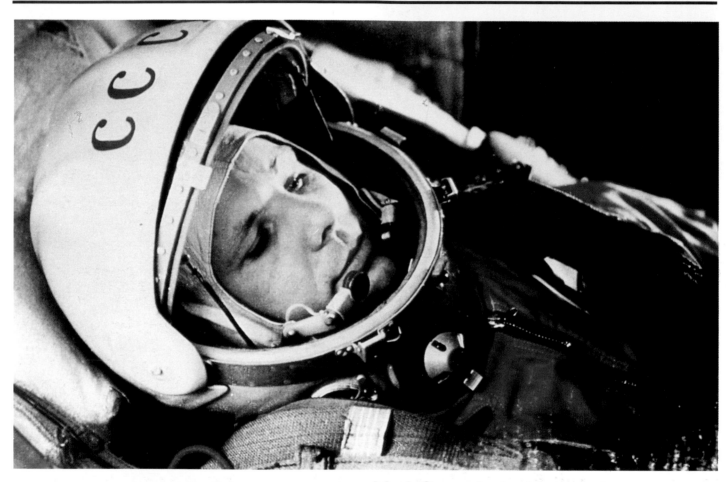

Yuri Gagarin in *Vostok 1*

Russian launched into space

April 12, Moscow, USSR The USSR has beaten the Americans in the race to put a human being into space. Earlier today, a Russian man landed safely after flying around the world in space. He is called Yuri Gagarin, and he is 27 years old. Gagarin made his flight in a spaceship called Vostok 1. The flight lasted 108 minutes.

Failed invasion at Bay of Pigs

April 20, Havana, Cuba There has been an attempt to invade the island of Cuba. Cuba has a Communist government led by Fidel Castro. Three days ago, 1400 invaders landed at the Bay of Pigs in Cuba. They wanted to defeat the Communist government. But Castro's troops have killed or captured all of the invaders. The Communist government of the USSR has accused America of helping the invaders.

British soldiers on guard in Kuwait

Arabs to guard Kuwait

September 19, Kuwait City, Kuwait Last July, British troops went to Kuwait in the Middle East. They were there to protect Kuwait from invasion by its neighbour, Iraq. Now, troops from Saudi Arabia and other Middle Eastern countries will take over from the British.

The space chimpanzee, Ham, and his nurse

News in brief...

Chimp in space

Jan 31, Cape Canaveral, USA American scientists have sent a chimpanzee into space. The chimp is called Ham. His flight lasted 18 minutes.

US troops in Vietnam

Nov 14, Washington DC, USA More US troops will go to South Vietnam. The US is worried about the Communists from North Vietnam who are moving further South.

1962

The Cuban missile crisis

October 25, Washington DC, USA Since the Bay of Pigs invasion, the USSR has been sending weapons to the Communist government in Cuba. Now, pictures from American spyplanes show that the USSR is building missile launch pads in Cuba. From these launch pads, the USSR could send nuclear missiles to hit the USA. Today, American navy ships have stopped 12 Russian ships from reaching Cuba. The Americans think that the ships are carrying weapons. Many people fear that this crisis could start a nuclear war between the USA and the USSR.

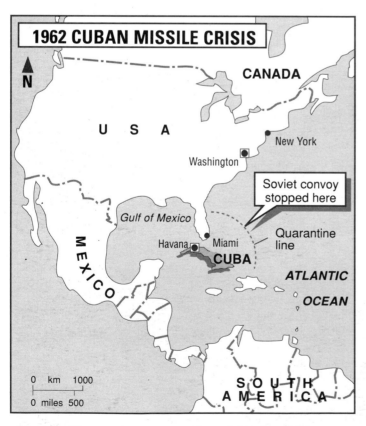

Cuba lies close to the USA. The US navy stopped 12 Soviet ships about 800 kilometres from Cuba.

On the edge of war

October 24, Washington DC, USA "I sat across from the President. This was the moment we had prepared for, which we hoped would never come... These few minutes were the time of greatest worry by the President. His hand went up to his face and covered his mouth and he closed his fist... We had come to the edge of a final decision, and the President agreed. I felt we were on the edge of a precipice and it was as if there were no way off."

(Robert Kennedy quoted in *Robert Kennedy and his times*, Arthur Schlesinger Jn., Andre Deutsch 1978)

Threat of nuclear war lifted

October 28, Washington DC, USA The threat of a nuclear war over Cuba seems to have gone. The Russians have agreed to destroy the missile launch pads in Cuba, and to take away all their weapons. In return, the Americans have promised not to attack Cuba.

African leader jailed

November 7, Pretoria, South Africa A court in Pretoria has sent the black South African leader, Nelson Mandela, to prison. He was found guilty of planning a national strike, and encouraging violent protests against the white government of South Africa.

Race riots in America

October 1, Oxford, Mississippi In the southern states of the USA, only white students are allowed to go to university or college. Black students are not admitted. But yesterday, a black man called James Meredith signed on as a student at a college. Thousands of white students rioted in protest. Three people died and over 50 were injured in the fighting.

Today, President Kennedy has sent a large group of police to protect Meredith in his college classes. But white students continue to protest. The riots have spread to other American cities.

Firefighters and police watch a meeting of black protesters in Alabama, southern USA.

News in brief...

First American in space

February 20, Cape Canaveral, USA The first American has travelled in space. He name is John Glenn. He flew three times around the Earth and landed in the sea near Puerto Rico.

John Glenn prepares to go into space.

Smog kills 60 in London

December 6, London, England Sixty people have died because of smog in London in the past three days. Smog is a mixture of fog and smoke.

A new cathedral

May 25, Coventry, England During World War II, German planes bomed Coventry. The bombs destroyed much of the city, and its cathedral. Today, a new cathedral stands in Coventry.

The inside of the new Coventry Cathedral

First hovercraft service

July 20, Rhyl, Wales The world's first hovercraft service began today. The hovercraft will cross the River Dee between Rhyl in North Wales and Wallasey in Cheshire. It can carry 24 passengers. A British engineer called Christopher Cockerell invented the hovercraft.

Marilyn Monroe dies

August 5, Hollywood, USA The film actress Marilyn Monroe has died. She was only 36 years old. She was found in her home with an empty bottle of sleeping tablets nearby. It seems that she took her own life.

Pop art

November, New York, USA Art critics are confused by a painting of a can of soup by Andy Warhol. Is this art or is it rubbish? The painting is called Big Campbell's Soup Can, 19c. This style of painting is called pop art.

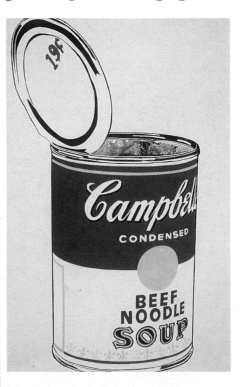

Andy Warhol's painting

1963

Kennedy shot dead

November 22, Dallas, Texas, USA President Kennedy is dead. He was riding in an open-top car through the streets of Dallas when someone shot him. His wife, Jackie, was sitting next to the president in the car, but she is unhurt.

Vice-President Lyndon B. Johnson will be the new president of the USA.

Oswald charged

November 22, Dallas The police have charged a man with the murder of President Kennedy. The man's name is Lee Harvey Oswald. Oswald used to be a marine in the US army.

Oswald shot

November 24, Dallas Someone has shot Lee Harvey Oswald. Police were taking Oswald to the county jail when a man stepped forward and shot Oswald. Oswald died instantly.

President Kennedy in his open-top car just before he was shot.

Murder mystery

November 26, Dallas, Texas, USA Police have charged Jack Ruby with Lee Harvey Oswald's murder. Jack Ruby owns a nightclub in Dallas. No one knows why he killed Oswald. And no one knows why Oswald might have killed the president either.

Jack Ruby shoots Lee Harvey Oswald

The world mourns Kennedy

November 25, Washington DC, USA People all over the world are mourning President Kennedy. Thousands of people stood silent on the streets of Washington as the body of the murdered president was taken to be buried. He will be buried in Arlington national cemetery.

Great train robbery

August 8, Cheddington, England A gang of robbers has stolen more than a million pounds. The robbery was well-planned. At ten past three in the morning, the robbers broke into a stopped train near the village of Cheddington in Buckinghamshire. The train was carrying a load of worn out bank-notes. The bank-notes were going to be destroyed.

At this bridge, the robbers loaded 120 mailbags on to a waiting lorry.

News in brief...

Scandal!

August 7, London, England A scandal is rocking the British government. The scandal involves the War Minister, John Profumo, a girl called Christine Keeler and a Russian diplomat. John Profumo has resigned from the government.

John Profumo

Death of Pope John

June 3, Rome, Italy Pope John XXIII has died. He was a very popular pope, because people felt he cared.

British railway cuts

March 27, London, England There is a new government report about the future of the railways in Britain. The report is written by Dr Richard Beeching. Dr Beeching thinks that over 2000 stations should be shut down. Many small towns and villages will lose their stations and railway line. Many people are angry about the cuts.

Beatles star in royal show

November 5, London, England 1963 has been the year of the Beatles! In April, the Beatles had their first number one hit. Their latest single is 'I wanna hold your hand'. It sold more than one million copies in only three days. Last night the Beatles appeared before the royal family in the Royal Variety Performance.

The Beatles: Paul, George, Ringo and John

1964

May 31   Palestinian Liberation Organization formed
August 5   USA bombs North Vietnam
August 10   Fighting stops in Cyprus
October 15   Khrushchev replaced
November 3   Lyndon B. Johnson elected US president

War in Vietnam

June 20, Washington DC, USA The American government is determined to fight Communism in South East Asia. Vietnam is the country most at risk. The USSR and China support North Vietnam, while the USA backs South Vietnam. Communist fighters, called the Vietcong, have taken control of large areas in the South. American soldiers are helping the South Vietnamese army to fight the Vietcong. But they are having little success.

A woman leaves her burning village in South Vietnam.

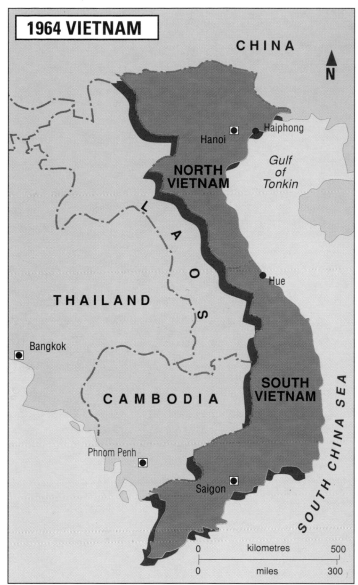

1964 VIETNAM

CHINA

N

Hanoi

Haiphong

Gulf of Tonkin

NORTH VIETNAM

L A O S

Hue

THAILAND

Bangkok

CAMBODIA

SOUTH VIETNAM

Phnom Penh

Saigon

SOUTH CHINA SEA

| 0 | kilometres | 500 |
| 0 | miles | 300 |

South Vietnam is threatened by the Communist North.

US bombs North Vietnam

August 5, Gulf of Tonkin, North Vietnam Ships from the North Vietnamese navy have fired on US ships. US aircraft have hit back by dropping bombs on naval bases on shore.

Johnson wins US election

November 3, Washington DC, USA Lyndon Johnson has won the US election and will continue to be president.

PLO formed

May 31, Cairo, Egypt Arab leaders are meeting in Cairo. They have agreed to set up a group called the Palestinian Liberation Organization (PLO). The PLO will help Palestinian refugees. The refugees left their home country when the state of Israel was formed.

Krushchev out

October 15, Moscow, USSR New leaders have replaced Khrushchev. The new leaders of the USSR are Leonid Brezhnev and Alexei Kosygin.

Nikita Khrushchev (left)

Lyndon Johnson

Turkey and Greece end war

August 10, New York, USA At the United Nations (UN) in New York, Turks and Greeks have accepted a plan to end the war in Cyprus.

Cyprus is an island in the Mediterranean Sea. The Turks and the Greeks both claim rights over the island.

Archbishop Makarios, the leader of the Greek Cypriots, in Cyprus

News in brief...

Clay wins title

February 25, Miami Beach, USA Cassius Clay has won the world heavyweight boxing title. He beat Sonny Liston. Clay says, "I am the greatest!" Clay is not only a good boxer. He also has a record in the pop charts.

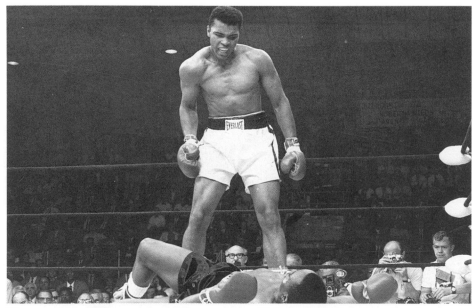

Cassius Clay stands over Sonny Liston during the boxing match.

Death of Nehru

May 28, New Delhi, India
India's Prime Minister, Jawaharlal Nehru, died suddenly yesterday. When India was a British colony, Nehru was a leader in the struggle for freedom. After India won independence from the British in 1947, Nehru led his country wisely. People in India and all over the world will mourn Nehru.

Nobel prize winner

October 24, Oslo, Norway
Dr Martin Luther King has won the Nobel Peace Prize for 1964. Dr King is the leader of the fight for equal rights for black people in the USA. This fight is often called the battle for civil rights.

The Tokyo Olympics

October 24, Tokyo, Japan
There was a double for Britain at the Tokyo Olympics when Mary Rand won the women's long-jump and Lynn Davies won the men's long- jump events.

Life for Mandela

June 14, Pretoria, South Africa A court in South Africa has sentenced Nelson Mandela to stay in prison for life. He is accused of plotting against the South African government.

China's nuclear bomb

October 16, Peking, China
The Chinese exploded their first nuclear bomb today. The USA, the USSR, Britain and France already have nuclear bombs.

Mary Rand won the gold medal for the women's long-jump event.

1965

Civil rights battle in USA

March 10, Selma, Alabama, USA There have been riots in the southern state of Alabama, USA. There has been a change in the law to allow black people to vote in elections. The white people of Selma are up in arms about the change.

Two days ago, police attacked a protest march of black people with whips and clubs. The black protesters were not being violent, but many were injured by the police. There is also news of other attacks on black people in several places in the southern American states.

A black protester is attacked by a white policeman in Selma, Alabama.

Civil rights march

March 25, Montgomery, Alabama, USA
Protesters have marched 80 kilometres from Selma to the capital of Alabama state, Montgomery. At the head of the march was the civil rights leader Dr Martin Luther King. Dr King delivered an appeal for equal rights to the governor of the state of Alabama.

Dr Martin Luther King leads the civil rights march in Alabama.

Victory for civil rights

August 6, Washington DC, USA
President Johnson has signed a new law that will give the vote to black people in America's southern states.

Race riots in Los Angeles

August 17, Los Angeles, USA There have been five days of race riots in Watts, a poor area of Los Angeles. Police had treated the black people of Watts badly. So they attacked white people and their property.

Rhodesians quarrel with Britain

November 11, Salisbury, Rhodesia
White Rhodesians are angry with Britain. Rhodesia is a British colony in southern Africa. The government of Rhodesia is made up of white people, led by the Prime Minister, Ian Smith. But Britain wants to organise an election and allow black people to vote. This would mean that there would be black people in government. Today, Ian Smith has declared Rhodesia independent of Britain.

The Rhodesian leader, Ian Smith

Britain blocks trade with Rhodesia

November 16, London, England Britain will not use force to end Ian Smith's rebellion in Rhodesia. Instead, the government will block trade with Rhodesia to try to make it impossible for the white government to run the country.

More US troops in Vietnam

December 31, Washington DC, USA President Johnson has promised that the Americans will not retreat or surrender in Vietnam. There are now 184,000 US soldiers in Vietnam.

News in brief...

Farewell to Churchill

January 30, London, England Winston Churchill died six days ago. He led Britain through World War II. He was also a reporter, novelist, painter, soldier and politician. Leaders from 110 different countries came to mourn at Churchill's funeral. The service was in St Paul's Cathedral.

Sailors march with Churchill's coffin

Short skirt problems

September, London Many schools will not allow mini skirts. Girls must wear a long skirt that will touch the ground when they kneel down. Boys are also in trouble for growing their hair long. The usual rule is hair 'above the collar'.

End to TV cigarette adverts

August 1, London, England The government has banned adverts for cigarettes on television.

Britain ends hanging

November 9, London, England From today, no one found guilty of murder in Britain will be executed.

1966

Chairman Mao's revolution

November, Peking, China The chairman of the Chinese Communist party, Mao Tse-tung, has started a new revolution. He believes young people must use violence to make China into an ideal Communist state. Millions of students have joined Mao's Red Guards.

Mobs of Red Guards have attacked their teachers and have forced people who seem to be well-off to work in the fields or in factories. They have destroyed old temples and works of art. Mao teaches that such things set a bad example in modern China.

Chinese protesters with a picture of Chairman Mao in London

War worsens in Vietnam

January 9, Saigon, South Vietnam The Americans are taking over in Vietnam. Until now, they have worked with the South Vietnamese army. But yesterday the Americans ignored their allies and attacked the Vietcong on their own. There are now 385,000 American soldiers fighting in Vietnam.

Nehru's daughter to lead India

January 19, New Delhi, India Indira Gandhi is to lead India's government. Mrs Gandhi is the daughter of Jawaharlal Nehru, the first Prime Minister of independent India.

The new Indian Prime Minister, Indira Gandhi

News in brief...

Gas in North Sea

December 12, London, England There is a huge amount of natural gas in the rocks under the North Sea.

Half-way!

January, Sydney, Australia Francis Chichester has sailed into Sydney harbour in his yacht, Gipsy Moth IV. He is sailing around the world alone, without any crew to help him. He is now half-way round.

Sailing into Sydney

Labour wins election

Harold Wilson (centre) with his ministers

April 1, London, England
The Labour Party has won the general election in Britain. The leader of the Labour Party is Harold Wilson.

Bobby Moore holds the World Cup.

England win World Cup

July 30, London, England
Today, the English football team won the World Cup. England beat West Germany 4-2 in the final at Wembley.

Leader killed with knife

September 6, Cape Town, South Africa A man has killed the South African Prime Minister, Dr Hendrik Verwoerd, with a knife. The man was white. He blamed the government for not helping poor white people in South Africa.

Dr Hendrik Verwoerd

Welsh school tragedy

October 27, Aberfan, Wales Six days ago, 116 children died in this small Welsh village. They were killed when a coal tip above the village slipped down the hill and covered the village school. Altogether 130 people died.

1967

Arabs attack Israel

April 30, Damascus, Syria Palestinian refugee fighters are regularly attacking Israel. The Palestinian fighters are based in Jordan and Syria. The Syrians also have guns on the Golan Heights overlooking Israeli villages on the plains below.

Egypt threatens Israel

May 23, Cairo, Egypt Egypt is moving thousands of soldiers and tanks to Sinai, close to the Israeli border. Egypt has also closed the Straits of Tiran to Israeli ships, so they cannot sail to the Indian Ocean.

Israeli soldiers on the march to meet Arab forces

Israel destroys airforces

June 6, Tel Aviv, Israel At breakfast time yesterday, Israeli planes attacked Egyptian airfields. The Israelis knew that most of the Egyptian planes would still be on the ground at that time of day. The Israeli planes destroyed most of the Egyptian airforce. In the afternoon the Israelis also attacked the airforces of Jordan, Syria and Iraq. On the ground, Israeli soldiers have attacked Egyptian forces in Sinai.

Egypt and Jordan stop fighting

June 7, Tel Aviv, Israel Israeli soldiers have taken control of Sinai. They have got as far as the Suez Canal. In the east, the Israelis have taken East Jerusalem and the West Bank area of Palestine from the Jordanians. The United Nations have put forward a plan to stop the fighting. Egypt and Jordan have accepted the plan. But the war between Israel and Syria continues in the Golan Heights.

Middle East fighting ends

June 10, Tel Aviv, Israel The Israelis have driven the Syrians out of the Golan Heights. Syria has agreed to stop fighting. Israel has won this six-day war. More than 100,000 Arabs have been forced to leave their homes and are now refugees.

Army seizes power in Greece

April 21, Athens, Greece A group of army officers has seized power in Greece. They have taken over from the government and put the leader of the government, Georges Papandreou, under arrest.

Sir Francis comes home

May 28, Plymouth, England Francis Chichester has returned home after sailing alone around the world. His journey took him 119 days and covered 49,000 kilometres. He returns as Sir Francis Chichester as the Queen has made him a knight.

Nigeria breaks up

May 30, Enugu, Nigeria The Ibo people have broken away from the country of Nigeria. The Ibo people live in the eastern part of Nigeria. The Ibo leader, Colonel Ojukwu says that the other Nigerian people want to kill the Ibos. So he has formed an independent state for the Ibos, called Biafra.

War in Biafra

July 31, Enugu, Nigeria Nigeria is at war with the state of Biafra. Nigerian soldiers are trying to reach the capital of Biafra, Enugu.

No end to war in Vietnam

November 21, Saigon, South Vietnam American aircraft continue to bomb North Vietnam. There are now over 450,000 US soldiers in Vietnam.

Many people in the USA want the Vietnam War to end.

With the Vietcong

December 10, near Hanoi, North Vietnam "Through the daylight hours nothing moves on the roads of North Vietnam, not a car nor a truck. It must look from the air as though the country has no wheeled transport at all. That, of course, is the idea, it is the roads and bridges that are being bombed...At dusk the roads become alive. The engines are started and the convoys grind away the rough the darkness behind the pin-points of masked headlamps... North Vietnam by day is abandoned; by night it thuds and grinds with movement."

(James Cameron from *What a way to own the tribe*, Macmillan 1968)

News in brief...

Oil covers beaches

April 2, Penzance, England Two weeks ago, a huge oil tanker ran aground off the coast of Cornwall. The oil spilt out into the sea. Now it has washed ashore, killing birds and fish and spoiling beaches.

The wreck of the tanker *Torrey Canyon*

A French-British project

The summer of love

September 1, London, England Last January, thousands of young people met in San Francisco to listen to acid rock bands. They called it the San Francisco 'Be-In'. Now the Be-In has come to Britain. A 'Festival of Love' was held at Woburn Abbey. Many young people came. They wore beads and flowers, and necklaces of silver bells.

The 'Festival of Love' at Woburn Abbey

First look at Concorde

December 11, Toulouse, France Today, the world has had its first look at Concorde. It will be the world's first supersonic aircraft – it will travel faster than the speed of sound.

Man given new heart

December 3, Cape Town, South Africa Dr Christiaan Barnard has carried out the first successful heart transplant. He has given a patient a heart taken from another human being.

Dr Christiaan Barnard

Campbell dies

January 4, Coniston Water, England Donald Campbell died today. He was trying to beat the world water-speed record on Lake Coniston. But his speedboat *Bluebird* went out of control and Campbell died.

1968

Martin Luther King killed

April 4, Memphis, USA Dr Martin Luther King is dead. The American Civil Rights leader was shot today. The killer shot Dr King while he was sitting on a balcony talking to friends. The killer escaped.

Friends join hands at the funeral of Dr Martin Luther King.

Thousands mourn Dr King

April 9, Atlanta, Georgia, USA Over 150,000 people came to Atlanta to mourn Dr Martin Luther King. Dr King's coffin passed through the crowded streets, lying on a wooden farm cart drawn by two mules. A recording of Dr King's last sermon was played at his graveside.

After King's murder

December 17, Washington DC, USA
After the murder of Martin Luther King in April, there were riots all over America. But today it seems that Dr King did not die in vain. Thanks to him and his followers, the law has been changed. Black Americans are to have the same rights as white Americans. Yet the struggle for black people is not over.

Bobby Kennedy shot dead

June 6, Los Angeles, USA Bobby Kennedy, the brother of the murdered president John Kennedy, is dead. Kennedy had just made a speech announcing that he would stand for president. A young Palestinian man ran up and shot him. The killer shouted, "I did it for my country!". Kennedy supported Israel in its war against the Palestinian people. This could be why he was murdered.

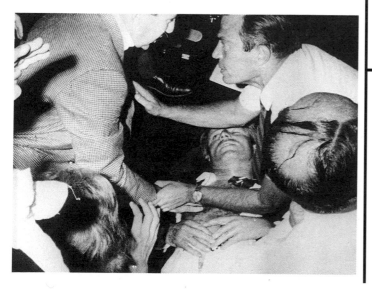

Rebels losing war in Nigeria

May 8, Lagos, Nigeria Nigerian soldiers have captured most of the main cities in the state of Biafra. The Ibo rebels are determined to fight on, although they have no chance of winning the war.

A rebel soldier in the state of Biafra

Nixon to be president

November 6, Washington DC, USA
Richard Nixon is to be the new president of the United States. Nixon has many problems to deal with including the Cold War, the war in Vietnam, and violence between blacks and whites in America's cities.

The Prague Spring

March 13, Prague, Czechoslovakia
Since the end of World War II in 1945, the USSR has governed Czechoslovakia. The Czech people have lived under the harsh rule of the Communists. But in this 'Prague Spring' there is new hope for the people of Czechoslovakia. The Czech government, led by Alexander Dubcek, has ended censorship. There is more freedom in Czechoslovakia than in any of the other Eastern European countries.

Alexander Dubcek

Russian tanks enter Prague

August 22, Prague, Czechoslovakia
Czechoslovakia is back under the control of the USSR. Russian soldiers and tanks have gone into Prague. The Russians have arrested Alexander Dubcek and his ministers. The Czech people are in despair. But they do not have the power to fight the Russian invasion.

News in brief...

First space man killed

March 27, Moscow, USSR
Yuri Gagarin died in a plane crash yesterday. He was the first man in the world to go into space.

Led Zeppelin in America

December 15, New York, USA The British band, Led Zeppelin, is a big hit in America. The group has stunned Americans with its powerful sound.

Led Zeppelin in concert

Circling the Moon

December 27, Cape Kennedy, USA A spacecraft carrying three American astronauts has circled the Moon ten times. The spacecraft came safely back to Earth today.

Black Power at the Olympics

October 27, Mexico City, Mexico Two American runners gave the Black Power salute during the medal ceremony at the Mexico Olympics. The Black Power salute is a clenched fist. Millions of people worldwide saw this protest on television. The runners have been sent home in disgrace.

1969

Flight to the Moon

July 16, Kennedy Space Center, USA At 9.32 a.m. this morning, Apollo 11 took off for the Moon. There are three astronauts on board Apollo. They are Neil Armstrong, Edwin 'Buzz' Aldrin and Michael Collins. Three thousand reporters and a million sightseers watched Apollo take off from its launch pad at the Kennedy Space Center.

"We have no complaints"

July 19, Houston Space Center, USA So far, everything has gone according to plan. The crew are pleased with the flight so far. "It was beautiful. We have no complaints," said Neil Armstrong yesterday. Neil Armstrong is the commander of Apollo 11.

Apollo 11 lifts off at the Kennedy Space Center, USA.

The lunar module approaches the surface of the Moon.

The Eagle has landed

July 21, Houston Space Center, USA The lunar module, called the Eagle, has landed on the surface of the Moon. Neil Armstrong reported back to Earth, "The Eagle has landed." Four hours later, Armstrong and Aldrin, put on their spacesuits. Armstrong was the first man to step on to the Moon.

Safely back to Earth

July 24, USS Hornet, Pacific Ocean The spacecraft carrying the three astronauts splashed down safely today. The spacecraft landed in the Pacific Ocean. An American ship, *USS Hornet* was in the Pacific ready to meet the spacecraft. President Nixon is on board the ship, ready to greet the astronauts.

Edwin 'Buzz' Aldrin walks on the Moon.

A view from the Moon

July 21, The Moon "The sky is black, you know... It's a peculiar thing, but the surface looked very warm and inviting." Neil Armstrong
"Still don't know exactly what colour to describe this other than greyish-cocoa colour."
Edwin 'Buzz' Aldrin
(From *First on the Moon*, Farmer and Hamblin, Michael Joseph, 1970)

Is it worth it?

December 31, Washington DC, USA Another spacecraft landed on the Moon last month. The astronauts collected 34 kilograms of Moon rock and brought it safely back to Earth. But sending spacecraft to the Moon is very expensive. Many people are asking, "Is it worth it?"

News in brief...

Czechoslovakia mourns

January 25, Prague, Czechoslovakia A young student called Jan Palach has burned himself to death. He was protesting against Communist rule.

Palach's grave in Prague

New leader for PLO

February 3, Cairo, Egypt The new leader of the Palestine Liberation Organization is Yasser Arafat.

Yasser Arafat

Oil under North Sea

June 25, London, England An oil company has found oil in the North Sea. The oil is in the rocks, deep under the sea.

Britain goes decimal

October 21, London, England In August 1972, Britain will change over completely to decimal coins. The new 10 pence coin came out last year. The seven-sided 50 pence coin comes out today.

People of the Sixties

John F. Kennedy 1917-63

John Fitzgerald Kennedy fought in World War II and won medals for bravery. He was elected president of the United States in 1960. He was admired across the world, and the whole world mourned when he was murdered in 1963.

Martin Luther King 1929-68

Dr King was a leader of America's black people in their struggle to win equal rights with white people. He was awarded the Kennedy Peace Prize and, in 1964, the Nobel Peace Prize. He was murdered in 1968.

Lyndon Baines Johnson 1908-73

Lyndon Johnson was Vice-President when J.F. Kennedy was killed in 1963. He became president, and was elected as president again in 1964. He was in power when the American government passed the laws to improve the rights of black people. But he became unpopular when the US did not win the war in Vietnam.

Nikita Khrushchev 1894-1971

Nikita Khrushchev joined the Communist Party in 1918. He became prime minister of the USSR shortly after the death of the famous Communist leader, Stalin.

Muhammad Ali 1942-

Muhammad Ali is a famous boxer. His original name was Cassius Clay. He changed his name when he joined the Black Muslim faith. He won the World Heavyweight Championship three times, in 1964, 1974 and 1978.

Alexander Dubcek 1921-92

Alexander Dubcek became leader of the government of Czechoslovakia in 1968. He introduced new freedoms to his country. But the USSR put an end to his reforms, and Dubcek was disgraced. He was honoured for his work in 1989, after the end of Communist rule in Czechoslovakia.

Indira Gandhi 1917-84

Indira Gandhi was the daughter of Jawaharlal Nehru. Nehru was the first Prime Minister of India after independence from Britain. Two years after the death of her father, Indira Gandhi became India's third Prime Minister. She was killed in 1984.

Billie Jean King 1943-

Billie Jean King is a famous tennis player. During her career she won 50 championships. She won 20 times at Wimbledon. When she became a top player in the '60s, men players were paid twice as much as women players. Billie Jean King fought for equal pay for women.

LIVERPOOL LIBRARIES & INFORMATION

For the first time ever

1960	USA	First vaccinations against measles
		Laser developed
	UK	Artificial ski slope opened
		First jump jet demonstration
	Japan	Fibre-tip pen on sale
1961	USA	Electric toothbrush on sale
		First electronic typewriter
	France	Hatchback car - Renault 4 - on sale
	UK	Toughened glass windscreen on sale
1962	USA	Telstar communication satellite
		Minicomputer on sale
	UK	Passenger hovercraft in use
1963	UK	Rotary lawnmower (Flymo) on sale
	USA	Navigation satellite launched
1964	USA	Eye surgeons use laser
		Music synthesizer in use
	Japan	Home video recorder developed
1965	USA	Global communications satellite
		Word processor available
	France	Radial tyre (Michelin) on sale
	UK	Pilots use automatic aircraft landing system

The pictures on this page show: Advert for film Lawrence
Artifical ski slope   of Arabia
Jump jet   Jaguar car
Renault 4   Polaroid camera

1966	USA	Every child wants a skateboard
	Japan	A supertanker is launched
1967	Germany	A car engine has fuel injection
	France	Tidal electric power station in operation
	South Africa	A human heart is transplanted
1968	UK	Astronomers discover pulsars
	USSR	Supersonic airliner flown
	Japan	Colour television developed
1969	USA	Jumbo-jet test flight
	Japan	Video-cassette system on sale

New words and expressions

Many of the new words and expressions which appeared for the first time in the '60s came from music, space travel, computers and war.

disaster area	networking
groupie	rip-off
hands-on	solar panel
hard rock	space shuttle
meltdown	space walk
microchip	update
mind-blowing	uptight
name of the game	world-class

How many of these words and expressions do we still use today? Do you know what they all mean?

The pictures this page 45 show: First man on Moon
Hovercraft   '60s fashion - the mini
electric till   skirt
Tidal electric power station   Jumbo-jet

Glossary

apartheid the law in South Africa that kept people of different races apart and did not give them equal rights.

Black Power the name given in the USA to the movement that fought for equal rights for black people.

civil war a war between people from the same country.

Cold War the name sometimes given to the hostility between the Americans and the Russians during the 1960s.

colony a territory governed by people from another country.

Communist a supporter of Communism. Communism is a way of organising society so that everything is owned by the community.

Cultural Revolution the revolution started by Mao Tse-tung in China. He believed that young people should use violence to make China into an ideal Communist state.

Eastern Europe the countries of Europe controlled by Communist governments.

nuclear weapon a weapon that uses the power of splitting atoms to explode. Nuclear weapons are very powerful.

Palestine the Arab name for a country at the eastern end of the Mediterranean. The Jews call it Israel.

PLO (Palestine Liberation Organization) a group set up by Arab leaders to help Palestinian refugees.

refugee someone who is forced to leave their home as a result of war or natural disaster.

superpower the Soviet Union and the USA were often called 'superpowers' because they were the two most powerful countries in the world.

supersonic faster than the speed of sound.

USSR (Union of Soviet Socialist Republics) this huge country extended from the Baltic Sea in the west to the Pacific Ocean in the east. The USSR broke up in 1991.

Index